FAMOUS FIGURES OF

CRAZY HORSE

THE AMERICAN FRONTIER

FAMOUS FIGURES OF THE AMERICAN FRONTIER

BILLY THE KID

BUFFALO BILL CODY

CRAZY HORSE

DAVY CROCKETT

GEORGE CUSTER

WYATT EARP

GERONIMO

JESSE JAMES

ANNIE OAKLEY

SITTING BULL

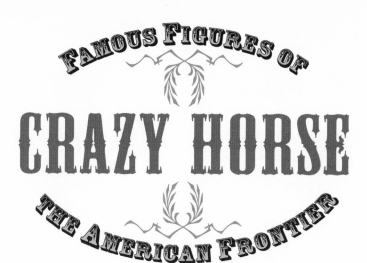

CRAZY HORSE

FAMOUS FIGURES OF THE AMERICAN FRONTIER

KRISTINE BRENNAN

CHELSEA HOUSE PUBLISHERS
PHILADELPHIA

Produced for Chelsea House by
OTTN Publishing, Stockton, NJ

CHELSEA HOUSE PUBLISHERS
Editor in Chief: Sally Cheney
Associate Editor in Chief: Kim Shinners
Production Manager: Pamela Loos
Art Director: Sara Davis
Series Designer: Keith Trego

First Printing

1 3 5 7 9 8 6 4 2

The Chelsea House World Wide Web address is
http://www.chelseahouse.com

Library of Congress Cataloging-in-Publication Data

Brennan, Kristine, 1969-
Crazy Horse / Kristine Brennan.
    p.   cm. – (Famous figures of the American frontier)
Includes bibliographical references and index.
    ISBN 0-7910-6493-X (alk. paper)
    ISBN 0-7910-6494-8 (pbk.: alk. paper)
1. Crazy Horse, ca. 1842-1877–Juvenile literature. 2. Oglala
Indians–Biography–Juvenile literature. 3. Oglala Indians–
History–Juvenile literature. 4. Indians of North America–
Great Plains–Wars–Juvenile literature. [Crazy Horse, ca.
1842-1877. 2. Oglala Indians–Biography. 3. Indians of North
America–Great Plains–Biography.] I. Title. II. Series.

E99.O3 C7217 2001
972'.004975'0092–dc21
[B]   2001028847

CONTENTS

Sundown

The guardhouse at Fort Robinson, Nebraska, where Crazy Horse lived in the spring and summer of 1877. In front is a memorial to the Sioux leader.

Late in the afternoon of September 5, 1877, an Oglala Sioux war chief named Crazy Horse rode into Nebraska's White River Valley. He was not alone: dozens of Indian scouts working for the U.S. Army rode with him. They were escorting Crazy Horse to Fort Robinson, part of Red Cloud *Agency*. Although he did not yet know it, Crazy Horse was under arrest.

After a long struggle, Crazy Horse had settled on Red Cloud Agency in May of 1877. The U.S. Army had been fighting to drive Native Americans onto *reservations*. The reservations contained agencies, which supplied the Indians with food and clothing in exchange for their freedom. Forts, manned by U.S. soldiers, were situated near the agencies to supervise the Indians. On September 4, Crazy Horse had left Red Cloud Agency because many people there wanted him dead.

Until this dark time, Crazy Horse was widely admired among his people, the Sioux. His valor in battle was apparent from an early age. As increasing numbers of white people invaded Sioux hunting grounds, Crazy Horse fought courageously to maintain control of the land. So great was his reputation that some Indians believed he was bulletproof.

Crazy Horse fought to remain free long after most of the Sioux had given up fighting the whites and had agreed to live peacefully on agencies. He had hundreds of followers who fought with him. But once the buffalo were slaughtered to near-extinction and the U.S. Army increased its efforts to drive Crazy Horse's people from their homeland, the Indians grew desperate. They were starving and weary. To save his followers, Crazy Horse moved them to Red Cloud Agency.

There, Crazy Horse's troubles multiplied. He was idle and unhappy at the agency. Although he had turned in his horses and guns when he came to Red Cloud, it was obvious to the white officers at Fort Robinson that he longed to be free. The soldiers regarded Crazy Horse with a mixture of curiosity, respect, and fear. They worried that he might cause trouble. But at the same time, many of them wanted to meet and talk to this chief who had fought so bravely for so long. The high-ranking officers at Fort Robinson wanted Crazy Horse to go to Washington, D.C., to meet with the president.

Red Cloud was a powerful and feared chief of the Oglala Sioux. Between 1866 and 1868, he directed a successful war against U.S. troops stationed in Montana. However, by the late 1870s, Red Cloud had agreed to move his people to the reservation in Nebraska named in his honor.

Crazy Horse received presents and attention as *inducements* to go.

Other Indians became jealous of the fuss whites made over Crazy Horse. They angrily whispered that if Crazy Horse went to Washington, he would be made chief of all the Indians on the agency. His simmering unhappiness with agency life made both Indians and whites afraid that he would stage a violent revolt. It seemed that nobody could relax if Crazy Horse was around. A group made up of white agency officers, mixed-blood interpreters, and disgruntled Indians plotted to kill him.

Crazy Horse went to another agency on the reservation, Spotted Tail Agency, looking for a safe haven. But he got a cold reception there. Even his own uncle, Chief Spotted Tail, the Brulé leader for whom the agency was named, seemed upset to see him. Spotted Tail feared that Crazy Horse's presence would disturb the peace. The Indian agent at Spotted Tail, Lieutenant Jesse Lee, convinced Crazy Horse to return to Fort Robinson. Lee promised Crazy Horse a chance to discuss his concerns with Fort Robinson's commanding officer if he went back the next day.

As he reached the parade grounds at Fort

Robinson, he saw hundreds of Indians and officers awaiting his arrival. A crowd formed around him. This must have made Crazy Horse–a loner by nature–very nervous.

What did they want from him? Crazy Horse's lifelong friend He Dog approached him. "Look out. Watch your step. You are going into a dangerous place," he warned.

He Dog's warning could not be ignored. The strange, solitary Oglala leader did not know what would happen next. Once, he had been free to ride like the wind across his ancestral hunting grounds. But now, his old life was becoming the stuff of history books as Crazy Horse dismounted from his pony in the fading sunlight at Fort Robinson.

FROM CURLY TO CRAZY HORSE

This 19th-century Currier and Ives lithograph shows a buffalo hunt on the Plains. The buffalo was very important to the Sioux way of life—its meat was used for food, its skin to make clothing and shelters, and its bones as tools.

Crazy Horse was born about 1840 in Bear Butte near the Belle Fourche River in South Dakota. He was a member of the Lakota Sioux people, part of the powerful Sioux Nation.

Crazy Horse was first known by his childhood nickname, Curly. His father was an Oglala holy man who was called Worm. His mother is thought to have been a

The three major groups in the Sioux Nation were the Lakota, Dakota, and the Nakota Sioux. There were four Dakota tribes, two Nakota tribes, and one Lakota tribe. The Lakota people were made up of seven smaller groups: the Oglalas, the Brulés, the Minneconjous, the Blackfeet, the Sans Arcs, the Two Kettles, and the Hunkpapas. Crazy Horse was an Oglala.

Minneconjou named Rattle Blanket Woman. She and Worm had an older daughter in addition to Curly. Rattle Blanket Woman died when Curly was about four years old. Worm then married two Brulé sisters: one of them was the mother of Curly's younger brother, Little Hawk.

From the start, the boy who would grow up to be known among the Oglalas as "Our Strange Man" was unlike anyone else in his tribe. Curly had light skin and brown hair. It was said that settlers traveling west along the Oregon Trail who saw Curly thought he was a white child whom the Oglalas had kidnapped. Crazy Horse's friend He Dog said that he was also called Yellow Fuzzy Hair as a boy.

Curly had an unusual personality to complement his appearance. He said little. Even after he rose to power, he was no *orator*. One French interpreter later remembered the Oglala war chief as "slow of

speech." Unlike many Sioux, who marked important tribal events by singing and dancing, Curly did
neither. The Lakota mourned the loss of their loved
ones by cutting off their hair and tearing their
clothes. Although Curly would suffer the loss of several loved ones as an adult, he would never show his
grief in these traditional ways.

Despite his strange ways, Curly probably played
the games Sioux children loved. He may have run
in footraces, gone swimming, or rolled hoops made
of branches with other children. Childhood was also
a time to learn responsibility. Before he was old
enough to hunt, Curly probably helped dig for wild
turnips and other roots to supplement the tribe's
main diet of buffalo, elk, and deer meat.

When he was about 11 years old, Curly probably witnessed a spectacular gathering of some
10,000 Plains people in Wyoming. The Fort
Laramie Treaty Council met in the summer of 1851
to *parley* with the U.S. government about the
Oregon Trail. The United States wanted to ensure
the safety of white settlers using the trail to reach
Oregon and California. The Indians had been
friendly to the first settlers, but now they suspected
that the *onslaught* of wagon trains was never going

Fort Laramie, Wyoming, was an important meeting place for both Native Americans and the settlers moving west, as this painting, made around 1847, shows.

to end. They responded by occasionally robbing or even killing the settlers.

The government wanted each tribal chief to sign a treaty promising safe passage for settlers along the Oregon Trail. In return, their tribes would receive $50,000 in goods annually. The government divided the surrounding land into separate tribal territories. Each Indian nation was supposed to select one chief for "all national business" with the whites. A Brulé named Conquering Bear was named head of the

Sioux. But it is doubtful that the Sioux took seriously the idea of a single chief leading everyone. Nor did they plan to observe the territorial boundaries set up for them. The settlers' troubles on the Oregon Trail were not over.

Curly learned to raid and hunt. His *mentor* was a Minneconjou named Hump. He made Curly's first bow and arrow and war club. Hump also taught his Oglala pupil how to scout for buffalo and for enemy tribes.

In the summer of 1854, Curly returned to the Fort Laramie area. He was staying near the Oregon Trail with his stepmother and her Brulé relatives. The Brulés were awaiting their goods from a government Indian agent in accordance with the 1851 Fort Laramie treaty. The younger Brulé warriors busied themselves harassing wagon trains along the Oregon Trail.

During his early teens, Curly started going on horse raids. Stealing horses from enemy tribes or white settlers was an important rite of passage into manhood for the Lakota. Curly proved so good at it that Worm changed his son's name to His Horse Looking (though this name never really caught on). The Crow and Pawnee peoples were frequent targets of Lakota horse raids.

On August 17, a party of **Mormons** was moving along the Oregon Trail. When one of their cows wandered into the Brulé camp, a visiting Minneconjou named Straight Foretop killed it with an arrow. The next day, the cow's owner went to Fort Laramie to complain to the supervisor, Lieutenant Hugh B. Fleming. Fleming called the Brulé chief Conquering Bear to the outpost and demanded that he turn in Straight Foretop for arrest. Conquering Bear refused to obey Fleming's order because as a Brulé, he did not believe he had any authority over a Minneconjou–even though the government considered Conquering Bear chief over all the Sioux.

Although he refused to hand over Straight Foretop, Conquering Bear did offer to give the cow's owner money or a good pony to make amends. Fleming refused the chief's offer. When Conquering Bear returned to his camp, he warned the Brulés to expect trouble.

Trouble came on August 19–in the form of 31 American soldiers marching toward the Brulé camp with a cannon and a mountain **howitzer** in tow. Leading them was John Grattan, a 24-year-old army lieutenant who was delighted at the chance to fight.

A half-drunk interpreter named Auguste Lucien, or Wyuse, didn't help matters by threatening the Indians. Conquering Bear offered Grattan a peace pipe; he offered one good horse each from five Brulé men to settle the dispute. Grattan was unmoved, insisting that Conquering Bear give up Straight Foretop—who hid among the warriors. After more than 20 minutes of fruitless talk, Grattan ordered his soldiers to shoot.

> While at Fort Laramie, Lieutenant John Grattan had bragged that he could whip the entire Sioux nation with 20 soldiers and a cannon.

Conquering Bear was mortally wounded. His warriors rushed Grattan's men, killing them all in minutes. Straight Foretop killed John Grattan. The Indians chased down Wyuse and killed him, too. The Brulés knew there was no way to make peace with the whites now. They fled the scene, taking their dying chief with them.

Curly left with the Brulés. But he soon drifted off by himself onto the prairie. Conquering Bear's violent death had disturbed him. It prompted him to wonder about his people's future, and his role in it.

Young men in Plains Indian tribes sought their destinies by going on *vision quests*. A vision quest was a period of fasting and praying alone. During that time, a boy would look for a sign or a dream to show him the direction his adult life would take.

Curly began a vision quest. He sat alone on the prairie for about three days with no food or water. He had skipped a few important steps, however. According to custom, Curly needed to perform certain ceremonies before seeking his vision. But he was doing things his own way, as usual.

Just as he was ready to give up because he had

These petroglyphs (rock carvings) from the Black Hills of South Dakota represent peyote buttons. Peyote is a drug that causes hallucinations. It was sometimes used by Native Americans who were undertaking vision quests.

not seen anything, Curly fell unconscious. A plainly dressed horseman appeared. He told Curly not to wear the fancy clothes that other men sported. The warrior told him to wear no more than a single feather in his hair—and never a war bonnet. But he was supposed to wear a small stone behind his ear. He was also instructed to throw a little dust over his horse before fighting. Most importantly, Curly was never to keep anything for himself. Bullets and arrows flew past the dream warrior without hurting him. But then one of the horseman's own people appeared and restrained his arms.

Soon after Curly's dream, Worm and Hump found him. They probably scolded him for taking off by himself. Curly kept his dream to himself for about two years. When he finally told Worm about it, the father put his son through the proper cere- monies. Together, they sought the vision again.

Worm helped interpret Curly's vision. Curly would be a warrior; but he was to avoid flaunting his prowess through ornate clothing or a feather bonnet. More importantly, his destiny would be to care for the weak, the hungry, and the poor—never keeping anything for himself. The battle Curly saw in his dream perhaps prophesied that he could only be killed if one of his own people held his arms.

Curly's vision demanded that he be at once warlike, humble, and generous. Could he live up to his vision during the hard times ahead? The buffalo herds that once covered entire prairies were dwindling. The Lakota not only had to compete for buffalo with their enemies the Crows and Pawnees, but also with whites—who frequently shot them for sport and wasted the meat. The growing scarcity of game had already driven some Native Americans to settle on reservations, giving up war and hunting for a steady supply of food and clothing.

But the greatest threat to the Lakota way of life was the United States Army. In the summer of 1855, General W. S. Harney led 600 soldiers on a mission to avenge the Grattan Massacre, as the whites called the fight that had taken place the previous summer. They found a village of Brulés led by Little Thunder living along the Bluewater River. On September 3, 1855, Harney and his men slaughtered about 90 of Little Thunder's people and took many prisoners.

Curly may have been staying with Little Thunder when the Bluewater Massacre took place. Many historians believe that he arrived at the Brulé camp to discover the bloodshed. He found a

Cheyenne named Yellow Woman still alive and returned her safely to her family.

By 1858, Curly dressed for battle as his vision instructed. He now wore a little brown stone tied behind his ear. He put only one feather in his hair. His vision had also indicated that he was immune to enemy bullets and arrows: to ensure this, he painted a single lightning bolt in blue or red on one cheek and spots on his body to represent blinding hail.

In the summer of 1858, Curly rode into Wyoming with his people to take Arapaho horses. Bullets and arrows whizzed past the young warrior as he rushed headlong against the enemy. When his horse was shot out from under him, he jumped onto a loose horse and kept fighting! He killed two Arapahos. But then he disobeyed his vision by dismounting and taking their scalps. He was promptly hit in the leg with an arrow. Hump cared for him and got him home safely.

Although he had foolishly disobeyed his vision and kept something for himself, Curly had won respect for his bravery. Back at camp, Worm sang to honor his son's courage and renamed him. The young Oglala would never again answer to Curly or His Horse Looking: he was now Crazy Horse.

WAR WITH THE WHITES

A determined Crazy Horse leads a Sioux war party in this painting by Guy Manning. Actually, no one is certain what Crazy Horse looked like—he would not allow anyone to photograph him.

Crazy Horse's reputation grew. In 1861, during a raid on the Shoshones near the Sweetwater River, Crazy Horse and his younger brother, Little Hawk, both lost their horses. A Sioux warrior named Short Bull later remembered that Crazy Horse told Little Hawk: "Take care of yourself—I'll do the fancy stunt!" He then yanked a Shoshone off his horse and jumped onto it himself. He got hold of a second horse for Little Hawk. Short Bull said that the brothers laughed as they raced to safety.

From 1861 to 1865, the U.S. Army was embroiled in the Civil War. While the United States devoted less energy to fighting Indians, Crazy Horse devoted his energy to courting a girl named Black Buffalo Woman. She was a niece of Red Cloud, the powerful leader of a group of Oglalas called the Bad Faces.

But Crazy Horse had a rival for Black Buffalo Woman: a proud man named No Water. In 1862, Red Cloud assembled a raiding party that included both Crazy Horse and No Water. Just before they left, though, No Water bowed out, complaining of a toothache. When Crazy Horse returned, he was crushed to discover that No Water had married Black Buffalo Woman.

He may have lost his one true love, but Crazy Horse was winning his people's confidence as a leader in battle. Crazy Horse was also a generous hunter, sharing his kills with the needy.

Although the Civil War distracted the army, there were still dark episodes in Indian country. On November 29, 1864, Colonel John M. Chivington and his 600 men killed more than 150 Cheyennes

Colonel John Chivington was a former minister and a Civil War hero. At dawn on November 29, 1864, his volunteer force swept down on the camp of Cheyenne Indians under Black Kettle, killing many of the defenseless men, women, and children—despite the American flag and white flag of truce that Black Kettle was flying over his tepee.

on Sand Creek in Colorado. Among the dead was Yellow Woman.

The Cheyenne chief, Black Kettle, led the survivors north to Sioux country near the Powder River. In December, Crazy Horse joined forces with them, along with other Sioux, including Red Cloud and the revered Sitting Bull, as well as Cheyennes and Arapahos. Thousands strong, the warriors attacked a stagecoach station in Julesberg, Colorado. Although the initial takeover of the Julesberg station and store took place on January 7, 1865, the Indians kept traders and soldiers there under siege until early February.

The Civil War ended in 1865. On June 13, Crazy Horse helped liberate about 1,500 agency Sioux who were on a forced march from Fort Laramie to a new agency at Fort Phil Kearny, Nebraska. Crazy Horse's party smuggled weapons to the captives, who then escaped and fled northward.

On July 25, Crazy Horse took part in an unsuccessful attack on American soldiers guarding the Platte River Bridge along the Oregon Trail. Although the combined force of Sioux, Cheyennes, and Arapahos greatly outnumbered the soldiers, the Indians were undisciplined and disorganized.

Perhaps to provide their young men with the leadership they seemed to need, the northern Oglalas revived an old custom. The Big Bellies, tribal elders over 40 years old, selected four outstanding young men to be Shirt Wearers. These men, who were responsible for maintaining order among the people, wore distinctive shirts. Crazy Horse was chosen to be a Shirt Wearer.

But it would take more than a special

Although Crazy Horse was known for his fearlessness in battle, he was not reckless. "He always used judgment and played safe," his friend He Dog later recalled.

shirt to save Crazy Horse's way of life. Gold had been discovered in Montana. The Bozeman Trail was bringing miners into the country to intrude on Indian hunting grounds. The U.S. government had called a failed peace council at Fort Laramie in 1865. Another council failed in 1866, when Red Cloud stormed out after learning that the government was building forts along the Bozeman Trail.

On December 21, 1866, Crazy Horse and a small group of warriors threatened some woodcutters outside of Nebraska's Fort Kearny. Captain William Fetterman was ready to fight. He hounded his commanding officer into letting him confront Crazy Horse's party. Crazy Horse and the decoy Indians led Fetterman and his 80 men on a chase away from the fort. Crazy Horse used *ploys* like pretending his horse was lame to lure Fetterman, who forgot his orders to stay within sight of Fort Kearny. The army captain pursued the decoys over a ridge. On the other side of the ridge, Hump waited with more warriors. When the Indians swarmed down on them, Captain Fetterman and all his men were killed in a matter of minutes.

The incident, dubbed the Fetterman Massacre, touched off Red Cloud's War—really a series of

General William T. Sherman and a U.S. peace commission meet with Sioux, Cheyenne, and Arapaho Indians at Fort Laramie. The 1868 treaty ended Red Cloud's War; in return Sherman promised to remove U.S. troops from several forts and allow the Sioux to hunt in the Powder River Valley.

battles for control of the Bozeman Trail. All of the Sioux and Cheyenne warriors who fought shared Red Cloud's determination to shut down Fort Kearny, Fort Smith, and Fort Reno. With no soldiers to guard the trail, the settlers would stop using it to enter the Powder River country. Fighting continued into 1868, until General William T. Sherman finally agreed to close the three hated forts.

This was only one condition of the 1868 treaty of Fort Laramie. The treaty also guaranteed the Sioux and the Cheyennes hunting rights to the land north of the North Platte River, between the Black Hills and the Bighorn Mountains. White *prospectors* were supposedly forbidden to enter this territory.

Red Cloud arrived at the treaty council on November 4. He brought 124 Sioux leaders with him. (Crazy Horse was not there.) All of them signed the treaty, but they may not have fully understood its terms. They could hunt on the land until the buffalo died out, but they were supposed to live on a reservation. The Great Sioux Reservation covered much of western South Dakota. Once an agency was built for them along the Missouri River, the Indians were expected to live there and send their children (ages 6 to 16) to a reservation school run by the whites, to encourage their "civilization."

As the Sioux faced increasing pressure to become "civilized," Crazy Horse would also face a series of personal hardships.

Despite the 1868 Fort Laramie treaty, whites continued to enter the Black Hills. The tension grew after gold was discovered there in 1874. The U.S. Army was sent in force to the area to protect the gold miners and settlers. A supply train for troops led by Lieutenant Colonel George A. Custer is pictured here.

HARD TIMES

In 1869, Red Cloud moved his Bad Faces to an agency named after him on the North Platte River. About half of the northern Oglalas joined him. Crazy Horse's uncle, the Brulé chief Spotted Tail, settled his people on the Spotted Tail Agency. Spotted Tail had seen the U.S. Army's power at the Bluewater Massacre, and believed he had to settle if his people were to survive.

Crazy Horse, too, had seen the bloody aftermath of the 1855 Bluewater Massacre. But unlike Spotted Tail, he continued fighting. However, he suffered a string of personal losses from 1870 to 1874 that made his ongoing pursuit of freedom more difficult.

During a raid on the Shoshones in early 1870, Hump took an arrow in the chest. Crazy Horse frantically tried to rescue his mentor, but a swirl of angry Shoshones surrounded Hump.

That summer, Crazy Horse caused his own problem. Although Black Buffalo Woman was married to No Water and now had three children, Crazy Horse was still enthralled by her. One day, when No Water was away, Crazy Horse rode off with Black Buffalo Woman and stayed with her in a friend's lodge.

No Water soon caught up with the runaway couple. When he entered the tepee where Crazy Horse was staying with his wife, he said, "Friend, I have come!" As Black Buffalo Woman scurried away, No Water shot Crazy Horse in the face at point-blank range. According to some versions of the story, an Indian named Little Big Man was also there, holding Crazy Horse's arms back as No Water approached. If this detail is true, it is consistent with Crazy Horse's vision.

No Water rode off in a panic, sure he had murdered Crazy Horse. He had nearly done so, but Crazy Horse eventually recovered. No Water made peace with Crazy Horse's people by offering Crazy Horse a good pony. Crazy Horse accepted, provided that Black Buffalo Woman was not punished. All Crazy Horse had to show for *eloping* with Black Buffalo Woman was a scar on the left side of his face. His poor moral example also cost him the privilege of being a Shirt Wearer. In fact, the whole Shirt Wearer tradition died out soon after this.

> Black Buffalo Woman's fourth child was a girl with unusually light hair. Some people gossiped that this child—who survived into the 1940s—was Crazy Horse's daughter.

Crazy Horse was probably still healing from his wound and his shame when he suffered yet another blow. Little Hawk, his brother, was shot to death in 1871 during a reckless attack on some gold miners.

Crazy Horse became increasingly solitary. The Brulé woman who had raised him encouraged a marriage with a woman in her late twenties named Black Shawl. "You must tell her there will be little joy in a life with me," Crazy Horse advised his stepmother. Black Shawl married him anyway. In the fall of 1871 the couple had a daughter named They Are Afraid of Her.

In August of 1872, a party of *surveyors* for the Union Pacific Railroad entered Sioux territory along the Yellowstone River north of the Bighorn Mountains. Some 400 troops guarded them. Among the soldiers was Lieutenant Colonel George Armstrong Custer. The Indians called him Long Hair because his blond curls flowed down from under his hat. Crazy Horse and the northern Oglalas joined forces with the great Hunkpapa chief Sitting Bull and his warriors to attack the troops. Some Cheyennes also joined them.

Crazy Horse supposedly baited the army's front line. Legend has it that Sitting Bull sat down on the battlefield and smoked a pipe as gunfire rained down. Despite such daring feats, the Indians accomplished little. Some young warriors died because they charged on the soldiers prematurely.

In the spring of 1874, Crazy Horse's fighting spirit temporarily left him. He returned from a raid against the Crows to find that They Are Afraid of Her had died. The cause of his daughter's death was probably an intestinal infection called *cholera*. She already lay on a burial *scaffold* far from camp by the

Sitting Bull was a powerful chief and medicine man of the Hunkpapa Sioux. In 1872 Crazy Horse joined forces with the other Sioux band to fight off the U.S. invasion of their territory.

time Crazy Horse returned. He took off on horseback and rode until he found her. They Are Afraid of Her lay wrapped in a red blanket, with her favorite toys beside her. Never one to display emotion in front of others, Crazy Horse remained with his little daughter's body for several days.

That summer, Custer went on yet another expedition into Sioux country—violating the 1868 treaty. This time, he was looking for gold. He was not disappointed. By August, Custer had told the press about a glistening bounty of gold just waiting to be mined from the Black Hills. He set the stage for the taking of the Sioux hunting grounds.

A Blaze
of Glory

This drawing of the Battle of the Little Bighorn was made by an Oglala Sioux named Amos Bad Heart Bull. A contemporary of Crazy Horse who was present at the battle, Bad Heart Bull's drawings were later published as *A Pictographic History of the Oglala Sioux.* Other drawings from this work appear on pages 45 and 55 of this book.

By 1875, the Fort Laramie treaty of 1868 had been violated numerous times. Now, the government wanted to buy the Black Hills from the Indians. The Lone Tree Council was a huge gathering of Sioux, Cheyennes, and Arapahos that met between the Red Cloud and Spotted Tail agencies. Neither Crazy Horse nor Sitting Bull attended, although Crazy Horse sent Little Big Man to observe. On September 20, the thousands of Indians in attendance were shocked to learn that the United States wanted not only the Black Hills, but also the land around the Powder River and the Bighorn Mountains!

The chiefs left the council wondering what to do. The council reconvened on September 23. Soon about 7,000 warriors stripped to *breechcloths* and wearing paint surrounded the council tent. Little Big Man stepped forward. He raised his rifle and screamed that he would kill the first chief willing to sell the Black Hills. Young Man Afraid, who had once been a Shirt Wearer with Crazy Horse, restored order. Red Cloud proposed that the Sioux ask for $6 million and *annuities*. In exchange, the whites could mine gold from the Black Hills. But the other chiefs did not support Red Cloud.

If the U.S. government could not buy the Sioux territory, it would take the land by force. On December 3, 1875, Commissioner of Indian Affairs Edward P. Smith declared that any Indians living off the reservations after January 31, 1876, would be considered "hostile." The military would be free to hunt them down.

The army prepared to attack the Sioux in

February. General Alfred H. Terry planned a three-pronged offensive. He and General John Gibbon would march east along the Yellowstone River from Montana's Fort Ellis; General George Crook would head north from Fort Fetterman on the North Platte River; Lieutenant Colonel George A. Custer would start at Fort Abraham Lincoln on the Missouri River and move southwest. The officers planned to surround the Sioux.

Crazy Horse noticed Crook's forces gathering along the North Platte that winter. Some of his followers fled to the safety of Red Cloud Agency before any trouble started. Crazy Horse led those who remained to join Sitting Bull's people at Chalk Buttes. That spring, they lived together in a huge encampment along the Rosebud River that held thousands of Sioux and Cheyenne patriots. Crazy Horse, by now an experienced war chief, regularly spied on Crook's men at Fort Fetterman. The Indians were prepared for war.

> In June 1876, Sitting Bull had a vision of U.S. soldiers falling upside down into the Sioux camp. This was considered to be a good omen.

On June 16, General Crook rode north from Fort Fetterman to initiate the army's attack. The Sioux and Cheyennes rode south to intercept Crook. The Battle of the Rosebud lasted all day June 17 with losses to both sides. Crazy Horse helped lead a counterattack that forced Crook to give up and turn his men around. The Indians were satisfied that they had won the Battle of the Rosebud. They moved their huge encampment to the Little Bighorn Valley in southeastern Montana.

A week later, Long Hair Custer led the Seventh Cavalry through the Rosebud Valley. He had 675 men with him, including his soldiers, civilian guides, and Indian scouts (Indians employed by the army to track down hostile Indians). Custer was looking forward to defeating the Sioux. Although his performance during the Civil War had made him the youngest major general ever, a feud with

When they saw the abandoned Sioux campsite, the Indian scouts who were with Custer's Seventh Cavalry prepared to die. The numerous imprints left by tepees on the ground and the large amount of droppings from the Indians' ponies indicated that the village was much bigger than Custer had expected. Two of Custer's scouts, an Arikara named Bloody Knife and a Crow named Half Yellow Face, warned the commander that they were doomed. Custer paid no attention to their warnings.

George A. Custer had been a hero during the Civil War. He had been promoted to general at age 25—the youngest general in the U.S. Army. Although after the war his rank was lowered to lieutenant colonel, Custer remained a popular figure with the public.

President Ulysses S. Grant had hurt his career. Now 36, Long Hair yearned to recover his lost glory.

Custer—who had cut his trademark long hair—kept his troops riding through the night of June 24. He wanted to charge the Indian village the next day. Custer disregarded an order to wait for Terry and Gibbon's forces to get into position. On June 25, he split up his troops, keeping about 210 men under his command. He sent Major Marcus Reno to attack the southern end of Crazy Horse's village with about 140 men. Captain Frederick Benteen led about 250 men north along a ridge that ran parallel to the huge Indian encampment, to scout the area. Custer rode beside Benteen's company for a short distance. Then he continued north along the Little Bighorn River, to the top of a hill overlooking the village.

According to a Cheyenne named Two Moon, the Battle of the Little Bighorn lasted "as long as it takes a hungry man to eat his dinner." When Reno charged the village at about three o'clock in the afternoon, as many as 2,000 Sioux and Cheyenne warriors were ready for him. After losing 40 men, Reno retreated to the top of a hill.

Custer realized that he had underestimated the Indians. He dispatched a note to Benteen requesting help and ammunition. But Benteen never arrived. Instead he joined Reno on the hill.

Custer and all of his men died on Last Stand Hill above the northern end of the village. Many historians believe Crazy Horse commanded approximately 1,000 warriors against Custer. Chief Gall—a Hunkpapa who lost two wives and three children in Reno's charge—vented his rage on Custer's men, running about 1,500 warriors right into them. Crazy Horse boxed the troops in when they tried to retreat from Gall's attack. In blinding dust and gun smoke,

Crazy Horse, pictured near the center of this drawing wearing a single feather in his hair, shoots down a Seventh Cavalry trooper during the Battle of the Little Bighorn. After dividing his soldiers, Custer led some 210 men north along the Little Bighorn River. When he was surprised by Chief Gall's force of about 1,500 warriors, Custer attempted to retreat, but Crazy Horse, leading 1,000 mounted Sioux, cut off his escape.

the Indians killed many of the soldiers with hatchets and war clubs.

Reno and Benteen survived the battle, holding off the Indians until General Terry's troops arrived. However, some 265 U.S. soldiers had been killed, while 100 Indians lost their lives.

The Battle of the Little Bighorn would be Crazy Horse's final taste of triumph.

The face of Crazy Horse begins to emerge from the Black Hills of South Dakota. The sculpture, which is still under construction, will be the largest in the world when it is finished.

FEAR AND LIES

On July 22, General William T. Sherman nullified the Fort Laramie treaty of 1868. The government forced agency Indians to sign a new treaty *ceding* all their hunting grounds to the United States. They threatened to withhold food from the Indians who did not sign.

General George Crook—still smarting from his defeat on Rosebud Creek—spent the fall of 1876 looking for "hostiles" in the newly ceded territory. On November 25, Crook attacked a Cheyenne village on the Powder River. The survivors struggled through the cold for three days to reach Crazy Horse's camp on the Tongue River. During the Cheyennes' flight to safety, 11 babies froze to death.

Crazy Horse did his best to help the survivors, although his own people were already suffering terribly. The winter of 1876-77 was bitingly cold, and game was scarce. In January, the U.S. military caught up with Crazy Horse. General Nelson Miles attacked Crazy Horse and his followers at Wolf Mountain, but the Indians escaped on January 8.

By spring, Crazy Horse realized that his people were doomed if he continued to resist the government. He reluctantly agreed to go to the Red Cloud Agency. On May 6, 1877, Crazy Horse led about 900 Indians into Fort Robinson, the military outpost housing the officers in charge of Red Cloud. Crazy Horse wore a plain shirt and leggings, with a single feather in his hair. He rode between He Dog and Little Big Man, both dressed in all their finery.

Red Cloud and 100 of his agency Indians met them a few miles outside Fort Robinson. The Red Cloud Indians offered them food and gifts from

Western artist Frederic Remington drew this illustration of General Nelson Miles's troops attacking Crazy Horse's village in January 1877. The attack actually took place at nearby Wolf Mountain.

Lieutenant William P. Clark. "All is well. Have no fear. Come on in," Red Cloud told Crazy Horse. Clark also rode out to receive Crazy Horse. He took the Indians' weapons and about 2,000 horses.

Some of the soldiers feared Crazy Horse would stir up a rebellion among the settled agency Indians. But Crazy Horse only wanted two things: to secure an agency for his people in a location he chose, and to be allowed to leave the reservation for a buffalo hunt. He had surrendered only after General Crook promised him both of those things.

While at Red Cloud Agency, Crazy Horse made a white friend. An army surgeon named Valentine McGillycuddy treated Black Shawl for *tuberculosis*. Dr. McGillycuddy admired Crazy Horse's bravery and concern for his people. Crazy Horse was grateful for the good care Black Shawl received.

Lieutenant Clark was supposed to make sure that Crazy Horse stayed put on Red Cloud Agency. Clark thought one way to keep Crazy Horse settled was to impress him with the power of white America. He wanted Crazy Horse to visit Washington, D.C., and meet with the president. But Crazy Horse refused to go until the officers at Fort Robinson kept at least one of Crook's promises.

Throughout the summer, Crook and Clark unsuccessfully urged Crazy Horse to go to Washington. Around this time, Crazy Horse took a second wife. She was a half-French, half-Cheyenne girl of 18 named Nellie Laravie (or Larrabee). Clark may have arranged the match to ingratiate himself to Crazy Horse.

But marrying Nellie may have added to Crazy Horse's problems at Red Cloud Agency. Rumors of Clark's involvement were thought to be proof that Crazy Horse got special treatment. Spotted Tail and

Red Cloud were particularly jealous. They feared that he was overshadowing their influence with the whites. Red Cloud and his followers convinced the officers at Fort Robinson that Crazy Horse was treacherous. If the whites gave him and his band guns and ponies for a buffalo hunt, they warned, Crazy Horse would use them to stage an uprising.

Crazy Horse never got his buffalo hunt. But the U.S. government had other plans for him. The military was trying to drive the Nez Percé Indians from Oregon to a reservation in Idaho. Clark wanted Crazy Horse and his followers to help the army conquer the Nez Percés. Crazy Horse was baffled. He had just given up his guns and ponies and vowed to fight no more—and now he was being drafted into a war! He reacted angrily:

> We are tired of war and talking of war! From back when Conquering Bear was still with us we have been lied to and fooled by the whites, and here it is the same, but still we want to do what is asked of us and if the Great Father wants us to fight we will go north and fight until there is not a Nez Percé left!

But Lieutenant Clark heard something quite different. An interpreter named Frank Grouard mistranslated the end of Crazy Horse's final sentence.

Grouard told Clark that Crazy Horse would go north and fight until there were no more whites left! Whether or not Grouard did this intentionally is still debated. Crazy Horse had been friendly with the interpreter in the past.

Another interpreter tried to explain Grouard's mistake, but Clark would not be appeased. Word that Crazy Horse had threatened the whites spread like wildfire around both the Red Cloud and Spotted Tail agencies. General George Crook arrived at Fort Robinson to investigate the trouble. He called the Red Cloud Indians to a council.

On September 2, 1877, General Crook was on his way to the council when an Indian scout named Woman's Dress stopped him. Woman's Dress warned Crook that Crazy Horse planned to shake his hand in friendship at the council, then kill him! Crook was skeptical, but other Indians assured him that Woman's Dress was right. Crazy Horse never even showed up at the council, however.

The storm of fear and lies surrounding Crazy Horse was gathering force. Lieutenant Clark, General Crook, and a group of interpreters and Indians that included Red Cloud met in Fort Robinson. They *conspired* in the apartments of

To entice Crazy Horse to settle on the Great Sioux Reservation, General George Crook promised the war chief an agency of his own. He also agreed to allow Crazy Horse and his followers to hunt buffalo outside the reservation. Crazy Horse became frustrated when these promises were not kept.

General Luther P. Bradley, the fort's commanding officer, who was not present. Clark offered cash and a fast horse to whoever murdered Crazy Horse. General Bradley soon got wind of the plot and ordered Clark to cancel it. Clark obeyed. But then Crook—who was Bradley's superior officer—ordered Bradley to arrest Crazy Horse.

Early on September 4, Bradley sent 850 cavalry soldiers and Indian scouts to capture the Oglala war chief. But Crazy Horse had fled for the Spotted Tail Agency upon learning about the plot against his life. He took his first wife, Black Shawl, but left young Nellie Laravie behind. Bradley's party soon took off in pursuit.

Crazy Horse reached Fort Sheridan (the fort at Spotted Tail Agency) just before his pursuers caught up with him. There, Indian agent Jesse Lee persuaded him to go back to Fort Robinson by promising him a meeting with General Bradley. Crazy Horse left Black Shawl with her mother, who was camped at Spotted Tail.

On the morning of September 5, Lee rode in a closed wagon to accompany Crazy Horse back to Fort Robinson. Spotted Tail, Touch the Clouds, and Indian scouts from Spotted Tail's agency rode with them. At one point, Crazy Horse galloped ahead and disappeared over a hill. He met an Indian family, who may have slipped him a knife. After the scouts caught up with Crazy Horse, Lee insisted that he ride behind the wagon the rest of the way.

Late that afternoon, a crowd watched Crazy Horse ride into Fort Robinson. He Dog warned him that he was in danger. Little Big Man—now an Indian police officer—and an officer named Captain James Kennington approached. Crazy Horse walked between Kennington and Little Big Man toward the guardhouse. It wasn't until they shoved him through the door that Crazy Horse realized he was being jailed.

This Bad Heart Bull drawing shows Crazy Horse being stabbed by a soldier outside the guardhouse at Fort Robinson. He is held by Little Big Man, wearing an Indian police uniform, and another Sioux.

He turned and sprinted back onto the parade grounds. Little Big Man grabbed Crazy Horse and tried to pin his arms. Crazy Horse produced a knife from beneath his blanket. He managed to cut Little Big Man's hand and break loose. A private named William Gentles bayoneted Crazy Horse. Two thrusts hit the chief.

Crazy Horse said, "Let go of me, friends. You've hurt me bad enough!" as he crumpled to the ground. For an instant the crowd forgot about Crazy Horse. It looked as if they would start shooting the soldiers and each other. But their attention quickly returned to the wounded man. He Dog covered Crazy Horse with his blanket. Touch the Clouds also rushed to help. Crazy Horse was carried into the *adjutant*'s office at around 5 P.M. He refused a cot, preferring to lie on a blanket spread on the floor. His friend Dr. McGillycuddy examined Crazy Horse and announced that he would die before morning. McGillycuddy could only ease Crazy Horse's pain with morphine as his life ebbed away. His father Worm was with him. So was Touch the Clouds.

How much Crazy Horse said as he faded in and out of consciousness is uncertain. At one point, Worm said to him, "Son, I am here," and Crazy Horse replied, "Father, it is no use for the people to depend on me any longer. I am bad hurt." But some say that he also summoned Jesse Lee at around 10 P.M. and made a long speech, forgiving Lee for what had happened. This speech exists in writing, but nobody can prove that the words are Crazy Horse's.

Worm and Touch the Clouds watched over him and wept. At about 11:40 P.M., Crazy Horse breathed his last. The wailing of Sioux women punctuated the darkness. The white officers feared that Crazy Horse's followers would kill them before morning. But morning came with no more bloodshed.

On October 27, 1877, the Indians from Spotted Tail and Red Cloud agencies reluctantly started east for their new agency on the Missouri River. It is said that his family slipped away somewhere in South Dakota and secretly buried Crazy Horse. Nobody has ever verified the location of Crazy Horse's bones.

There are no confirmed photos of Crazy Horse, either.

The Sioux grieved for the death of Crazy Horse. An Indian named Red Feather, the brother of Crazy Horse's wife Black Shawl, later said that a spotted eagle landed on the war chief's coffin each night.

He never allowed anyone to take his picture. But his face now stands nine stories tall on Thunderhead Mountain in Custer, South Dakota. A sculptor named Korczak Ziolkowski began coaxing Crazy Horse's form out of the rock in the 1940s. After Ziolkowski died in 1982, his children took over. When the Crazy Horse sculpture is finished, it will be the largest in the world.

The events of Crazy Horse's life and death are shrouded in legend, but it is certain that he deserves an honored place in American history as a symbol of hope, determination, and courage against overwhelming odds.

CHRONOLOGY

1840? Crazy Horse, whose childhood nickname will be Curly, is born in Bear Butte in South Dakota

1851 Probably attends Fort Laramie Treaty Conference in Wyoming

1854 Witnesses Grattan Massacre on August 19; receives vision that he will be a warrior who helps and defends his people

1855 Rescues Yellow Woman after Bluewater Massacre on September 3

1858 Renamed Crazy Horse after courageous performance in battle

1865 Fights in combined force of Sioux, Cheyennes, and Arapahos, attacking Julesberg, Colorado, stagecoach station and store on January 7; helps liberate captive agency Sioux on June 13; fights in Battle of the Platte River Bridge on July 25

1866 Helps lead Captain William Fetterman and his troops into a disastrous ambush, later called the Fetterman Massacre, on December 21; Red Cloud's War begins

1868 Sioux chiefs sign treaty guaranteeing them hunting rights in the Black Hills and the Powder River country to end Red Cloud's War

1870 Crazy Horse's mentor Hump is killed during a raid against the Shoshones; Crazy Horse is wounded by No Water after eloping with Black Buffalo Woman

1871 Loses brother, Little Hawk; marries Black Shawl; daughter They Are Afraid of Her born

1872 Joins Sitting Bull to attack Northern Pacific Railroad surveyors invading Sioux territory

1874 They Are Afraid of Her dies; George Armstrong Custer invades Black Hills and finds gold

1875 U.S. government fails to purchase Sioux territory at Lone Tree Council and decides to take it instead; orders Indians onto reservations

1876 Crazy Horse joins Sitting Bull and helps gather a large Sioux and Cheyenne force; General George Crook is defeated at the Battle of the Rosebud on June 17; Custer and his Seventh Cavalry troops are destroyed in Battle of the Little Bighorn on June 25

1877 Crazy Horse surrenders at Fort Robinson on May 6; he is killed there on September 5

GLOSSARY

adjutant–a staff officer who assists a commanding officer in the army or another branch of the armed forces.

agency–a central area on a reservation, from which the reservation was governed, and food or clothing distributed to the Native Americans living there.

annuity–a sum of money paid annually.

breechcloth–a cloth worn around the waist that covers the crotch; also called a loincloth.

cede–to yield or grant something, such as land, according to a treaty or agreement.

cholera–an infectious disease that produces acute diarrhea and spreads especially where sanitation is poor.

conspire–to work together with others in planning a wrongful or unlawful act; to scheme or plot against someone.

elope–to run away from one's husband with a lover; to run away secretly with the intention of getting married.

howitzer–a type of short cannon.

inducement–something that influences or persuades a person to follow a particular course of action.

mentor–a trusted counselor or guide, especially an older person who helps a younger person.

Mormons–members of a religious sect established in 1830 by Joseph Smith. During the 1840s and 1850s, many Mormons moved westward, eventually settling in Utah.

onslaught–an especially fierce attack, or something that resembles one.

orator–a person known for his or her ability as a public speaker.

parley–to meet and speak with an enemy.

ploy–a tactic designed to mislead or frustrate an opponent.

prospectors–people searching for valuable minerals, such as gold.

reservation–a piece of public land set aside where Native Americans were forced to live.

scaffold–a platform.

surveyors–people whose job it is to determine the form and extent of an area of land.

tuberculosis–an often deadly disease that affects the lungs.

vision quest–a Native American custom by which a young person, through several days of fasting, prayer, and isolation, seeks a vision about the shape of his or her adult life.

FURTHER READING

Connell, Evan S. *Son of the Morning Star: Custer and the Little Bighorn.* San Francisco: North Point Press, 1984.

Frazier, Ian. *Great Plains.* New York: Farrar, Straus & Giroux, 1989.

Guttmacher, Peter. *Crazy Horse.* New York: Chelsea House Publishers, 1994.

Hardorff, Richard G., ed. *The Surrender and Death of Crazy Horse.* Spokane, Wash.: The Arthur H. Clark Company, 1998.

Jordan, Robert Paul. "Ghosts on the Little Bighorn." *National Geographic,* December 1986.

Manning, Richard. *Grassland.* New York: Viking, 1995.

McMurtry, Larry. *Crazy Horse.* New York: Penguin Putnam Inc., 1999.

Sandoz, Mari. *Crazy Horse: Strange Man of the Oglalas.* New York: Knopf, 1941.

PICTURE CREDITS

KRISTINE BRENNAN is a writer and editor in the Philadelphia area, where she lives with her husband and sons. She holds a B.A. in English with a concentration in professional writing from Elizabethtown College. This is her sixth book for Chelsea House.